Sports Illustrated KIDS
STARS OF SPORTS

T0008778

SHOHEI OHTANI

BASEBALL TRAILBLAZER

■■▮▮ by Cheryl Kim

CAPSTONE PRESS
a capstone imprint

Published by Capstone Press, an imprint of Capstone
1710 Roe Crest Drive, North Mankato, Minnesota 56003
capstonepub.com

Library of Congress Cataloging-in-Publication Data
Names: Kim, Cheryl, author.
Title: Shohei Ohtani : baseball trailblazer / by Cheryl Kim.
Description: North Mankato, Minnesota : Capstone Press, 2024. | Series: Sports illustrated kids stars of sports | Includes bibliographical references and index. | Audience: Ages 8 to 11 | Audience: Grades 4-6 | Summary: " Shohei Ohtani has turned heads as the first professional baseball player since Babe Ruth to both pitch and hit. His speed, skill, and strength has made him a beloved player around the world. Find out more about his journey from growing up in Japan to becoming a worldwide baseball superstar"— Provided by publisher.
Identifiers: LCCN 2022050162 (print) | LCCN 2022050163 (ebook) | ISBN 9781669018193 (hardcover) | ISBN 9781669018148 (paperback) | ISBN 9781669018155 (pdf) | ISBN 9781669018179 (kindle edition) | ISBN 9781669018186 (epub)
Subjects: LCSH: Ohtani, Shohei, 1994- —Juvenile literature. | Pitchers (Baseball)—United States—Biography—Juvenile literature. | Pitchers (Baseball)—Japan—Biography—Juvenile literature.
Classification: LCC GV865.O42 K56 2024 (print) | LCC GV865.O42 (ebook) | DDC 796.357092 [B]—dc23/eng/20221020
LC record available at https://lccn.loc.gov/2022050162
LC ebook record available at https://lccn.loc.gov/2022050163

Editorial Credits
Editor: Mandy Robbins; Designer: Hilary Wacholz; Media Researcher: Jo Miller; Production Specialist: Tori Abraham

Image Credits
Alamy: Aflo Co. Ltd., 5, 15, 17, Glasshouse Images, 23, REUTERS, 12, 13, 24; Getty Images: Diamond Images, 28, Kevork Djansezian, 19, Kyodo News, 21, 26, 27, The Asahi Shimbun, 9, 10, 11; Newscom: Kyodo, 7, Kyodonews/ZUMAPRESS, cover; Shutterstock: Adam Vilimek, 1, image_vulture, 25, Michael Kraus, 20; Sports Illustrated/SI Cover, 22

Source Notes
Pg. 6: "Before high school . . ." Arden Zwelling, "The Next Babe Ruth," SportsNet, https://www.sportsnet.ca/baseball/mlb/big-read-meet-shohei-otani-next-babe-ruth/, accessed October 10, 2022.
Pg. 8: "The mound is . . ." Corinne Purtill, "The Case for Giving Grunt Work to Your Organization's Biggest Stars," Quartz at Work, October 26, 2017, https://qz.com/work/1103897/the-case-for-giving-grunt-work-to-your-organizations-biggest-stars/, accessed October 10, 2022.
Pg. 9: "It's been my dream" Mark Feinsand, New York Daily News, "Yankees Intrigued by Shohei Otani, Japanese Teenager with 100 MPH Fastball . . ." October 22, 2012, https://www.nydailynews.com/sports/baseball/yankees/yanks-intrigued-japanese-teen-phenom-100-mph-fastball-article-1.1189826, accessed October 10, 2022.
Pg. 12: "He was always doing extra work . . ." Ben Lindbergh, The Ringer.com, "Inside Shohei Ohtani's Superhero Origin Story," July 12, 2021, https://www.theringer.com/mlb/2021/7/12/22573272/shohei-ohtani-first-two-way-season-nippon-ham-fighters, accessed December 6, 2022.
Pg. 13: "Growing up, I watched Ichiro. . ." ALTHON Sports, "Shohei Ohtani: MLB's Greatest Sho on Earth in 2021," March 30, 2022, https://athlonsports.com/mlb/shohei-ohtani-mlbs-greatest-sho-earth-2021, accessed October 11, 2022.
Pg.14: "Without those struggles . . ." Kyle Glaser, Baseball America, "2018 MLB Rookie Of The Year: Shohei Ohtani," October 4, 2018, https://www.baseballamerica.com/stories/2018-mlb-rookie-of-the-year-shohei-ohtani/, accessed October 11, 2022.
Pg. 16: "He's beyond talented . . ." Eric Stephen, Halos Heaven, "2020 Angels in Review: Shohei Ohtani," December 21, 2020, https://www.halosheaven.com/2020/12/21/22193524/shohei-ohtani-angels-2020-review, accessed October 11, 2022.
Pg. 18: "I'm grateful for the awards . . ." Antoni Slodkowski, Reuters, "Japan's MLB Star Ohtani 'Grateful' For Big Season Despite Challenges," https://www.reuters.com/lifestyle/sports/baseball-japans-mlb-star-ohtani-grateful-big-season-despite-challenges-2021-11-15/, accessed October 11, 2022.
Pg. 22: "More than pressure . . ." Scooby Axson, USA TODAY, "Shohei Ohtani Talks Baseball Superstardom, Stephen A. Smith Criticisms in GQ Article," January 12, 2022, https://www.usatoday.com/story/sports/mlb/angels/2022/01/12/shohei-ohtani-face-baseball/9185957002/, accessed October 11, 2022.
Pg. 24: "Not only is he incredible . . ." Alex Rodriguez, TIME mazazine, "THE 100 MOST INFLUENTIAL PEOPLE OF 2021: Shohei Ohtani," September 15, 2021, https://time.com/collection/100-most-influential-people-2021/6096102/shohei-ohtani/, accessed October, 11, 2022.
Pg. 26: "Shohei did something . . ." City News Service, Spectrum News 1, "The Angels Hope 'Ohtani Mania' Brings Fans to the Ballpark," April 7, 2022, https://spectrumnews1.com/ca/la-west/sports/2022/04/07/the-angels-hope-ohtani-mania-brings-fans-to-the-ballpark, accessed October 11, 2022.
Pg. 28: "The only thing I can promise you . . ." Sports Biographies, "Shohei Ohtani Biography–Angels Star from Humble Beginnings," April 20, 2018, https://biography558972996.wordpress.com/2018/04/20/the-journey-begins/, accessed October 11, 2022.

All internet sites appearing in back matter were available and accurate when this book was sent to press.

TABLE OF CONTENTS

Words in **BOLD** are in the glossary.

A TWO-WAY PLAYER

During his long-awaited **debut** in Major League Baseball (MLB), Shohei Ohtani stepped up to the plate. On his very first pitch, Ohtani launched the ball into right field. He sprinted to first base—safe! Three days later, Ohtani stepped up to the mound. He checked the catcher's sign. He lifted his leg and wound up. Ohtani released the ball at almost 100 miles per hour (mph)! In six innings, he only allowed three runs. The Angels won the series! Ohtani became the first player since 1919 to both bat and pitch within the first 10 games.

The Angels' next game was against the Chicago White Sox. Ohtani stepped up to bat again. Crack! He sent the ball flying out of the park for a three-run homer. The crowd leapt to their feet! Ohtani waved his helmet as the crowd cheered on.

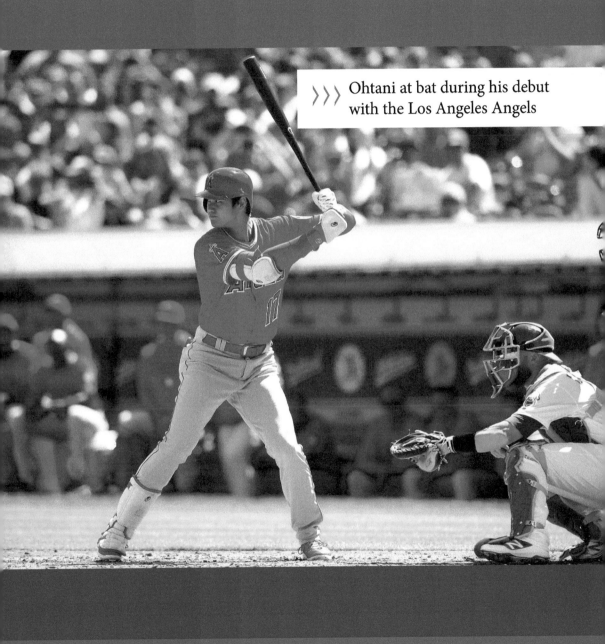

>>> Ohtani at bat during his debut with the Los Angeles Angels

CHAPTER ONE
HUMBLE BEGINNINGS

Shohei Ohtani was born on July 5, 1994, in Mizusawa, Japan. Today the city is called Ōshū. Shohei's father, Toru, played baseball for a corporate league. His mother, Kayoko, played badminton.

As a young child, Ohtani enjoyed trying new things on the playground. After watching a baseball game in second grade, Ohtani wanted to play that sport too. He practiced by playing catch with his dad and brother, Ryuta.

In middle school, Ohtani joined the Ichinoseki Little Senior baseball association. His dad also helped to coach the club. Ohtani only played on the weekends. "Before high school, I didn't participate in many tournaments," said Ohtani. "So I assumed there must be many players better than me."

母の日おめでとうございます。

Shohei Ohtani & Mom

>>> A photo of young Shohei Ohtani and his mother on the big screen in Angel Stadium on Mother's Day 2021.

FACT

Horace Wilson was an American living in Japan. He first introduced baseball in Japan as a school sport in 1872.

As a teenager, Ohtani attended Hanamaki Higashi High School in Iwate Prefecture, Japan. Baseball students were **recruited** and lived on campus. His coach assigned chores to all the players. Ohtani and the other pitchers scrubbed toilets. According to Coach Hiroshi Sasaki. "The mound is the most elevated place on the field," and "Scrubbing the dorm's humblest appliance keeps egos in check."

By age 16, Ohtani stood well over 6 feet (183 centimeters) tall. His pitches were in the mid-90 mph range. During a tournament just before he turned 18, Ohtani pitched a 99 mph fastball! Soon, scouts for MLB teams had their eyes on him.

FACT

Japan has 47 prefectures. These areas have their own governments that rank just below the national Japanese government.

Ohtani wanted to go straight to the MLB from high school. People thought he might be the first Japanese player to do so. "It's been my dream to play in the majors since I started school," said Ohtani.

>>> Ohtani pitching for his high school team

CHAPTER TWO

JAPAN'S ALL STAR

Right after high school, Ohtani came close to signing with an MLB team. He would have started in the minor leagues as a pitcher. At the same time, Ohtani was offered a deal from the Hokkaido Nippon-Ham Fighters. It was one of Japan's top baseball league teams. They wanted Ohtani to pitch and hit. Never before had a pitcher also been a hitter in the Nippon Professional Baseball Organization (NPB). Ohtani accepted the offer. "I feel like it brings out my unique rhythm," Ohtani said.

>>> Ohtani's press conference after signing with the Nippon-Ham Fighters

Surprisingly, Ohtani played his first professional game not as a pitcher, but as a right fielder. He was just 18. During his **rookie** season, Ohtani pitched 13 of the 77 games he played. His batting average was .238, including three home runs. He also pitched in 13 games, with an earned run average (ERA) of 4.23. Ohtani spent five years in the NPB with the Nippon-Ham Fighters.

〉〉〉 Ohtani hits a double during his second game with the Nippon-Ham Fighters.

During his time in the NPB, Ohtani improved. He worked on building muscle and strength. He went from 190 pounds to 210 pounds. He became a home run hitter. In 2016, he finished with a 1.86 ERA and hit 22 home runs. He led his team to the series championship. He was named the NPB Pacific League's best pitcher and best designated hitter of the year!

Ohtani's character also stood out on the field. "Just had his nose to the grindstone, always doing extra work, and always doing it with a smile on his face," said Ken Iwamoto, a Fighters staff member. "He was so humble. From the first day on, he never changed."

>>> Hideki Matsui

Notable Japanese MLB Players

Since 1964, 64 Japanese NPB players have joined the MLB . Ohtani's childhood baseball hero, Hideki Matsui, played for the New York Yankees. He was the first Yankee to hit a grand slam in his first game. In 2009, he won the World Series with the Yankees and was named the World Series Most Valuable Player (MVP).

Ichiro Suzuki, an outfielder, played professional baseball in Japan and the United States for a combined 28 seasons. He was a 10-time Gold Glove winner. The Gold Glove is given to the best defenders at each position in each league. In 2022, Suzuki was **inducted** into the Seattle Mariners' Hall of Fame. "Growing up, I watched Ichiro, and he won MVP, and it got me wanting to play in the big leagues someday," says Ohtani, through an interpreter. "Hopefully, I can be that kind of figure to the kids watching me right now."

CHAPTER THREE

MLB POWERHOUSE

In 2017, Ohtani became a **free agent**. All 30 MLB teams wanted to sign him. He ended up signing with the Los Angeles Angels. The Angels agreed to let Ohtani pitch and bat on his pitching off days. He would be the first two-way MLB player in almost 100 years.

Expectations were high. During spring training, Ohtani struggled. People questioned whether he should start in the majors. Once the season started, Ohtani rose to the challenge. In his first week, he pitched six strong innings with his fast ball reaching 99.6 mph. He went on to hit a home run in each of the next three games. With more standout performances, Ohtani was voted MLB Rookie of the Year. "Without those struggles, maybe I wouldn't have had success this year," said Ohtani. "I tried to take positive stuff out of it."

›› › Ohtani shakes hands with Angels manager Mike Scioscia after signing with the team.

In 2018, Ohtani tore a **ligament** in his elbow. He underwent Tommy John elbow surgery. The next season, Ohtani only played as a hitter. He also missed the last three weeks due to a knee injury. In 2020, the **COVID-19 pandemic** shortened the season. Still **rehabbing** from his injuries, Ohtani only played in 46 games. "He's beyond talented," said general manager Perry Minasian. "He can do things that 99 percent of the people can't. But this is a hard game . . . He's a young player going through ups and downs early in his career."

Ohtani felt frustrated with his performance. It pushed him to work harder in the off season. He made changes to his diet. He practiced hitting against a live pitcher. Ohtani also visited the Driveline Baseball facility in Seattle. The center uses data to create individual development programs for its players.

FACT

Pitcher Tommy John had surgery for a torn ligament in his elbow in 1974. He was the first person to do so and successfully return to the MLB.

>>> Ohtani wears an elbow brace at practice while recovering from Tommy John surgery.

CHAPTER FOUR

ONCE-IN-A-LIFETIME PLAYER

In 2021, MLB changed a rule. It used to be that a pitcher could not hit after he'd been taken out of the game. But now, when starting pitchers are taken out of a game, they can still be in the batting line up. Because of this, Ohtani shattered records. He had 156 strikeouts over 130 innings on the mound. He hit 46 home runs and 100 runs batted in (RBIs) at the plate. He was the fastest base runner in the American League. He also made history by being the first MLB player to play in the All-Star Game as both a pitcher and a batter. He received the American League Outstanding Player of the Year award and was **unanimously** voted American League MVP.

While Ohtani appreciates the recognition, he always wants to improve his game. "I'm grateful for the awards," he has said, "but personally, I'm already thinking about how I can play well so that I can receive these kinds of awards next season too."

>>> Ohtani pitching on April 4, 2021 at an Angels home game

In 2022, Ohtani hit his first grand slam! It led to an 11-3 win against the Tampa Bay Rays. On June 9, Ohtani helped end a 14-game losing streak. He gave up only one run in seven innings. His fastball reached 101 mph. He hit a two-run home run. The Angels beat the Boston Red Sox 5-2.

FACT

The Angels created Ohtani Rules, which kept him from batting on days before or after he pitched. This limited Ohtani. In 2021, the rules were thrown out, allowing Ohtani to play more.

>>> Ohtani hits his first grand slam on May 9, 2022.

In 2022, Ohtani was on the cover of *TIME* magazine. He was only the second MLB player to be on the cover since 2004. That same year, Ohtani was the cover choice for the video game *MLB The Show*. He was the first Angels player to be featured on the cover. Ohtani also appeared in two different covers, as a pitcher and batter, for *Sports Illustrated* magazine.

When asked if he felt pressure to be the face of baseball, Ohtani said, "More than pressure, I'm actually happy to hear that. It's what I came here for, to be the best player I can. And hearing 'the face of baseball,' that's very welcoming to me."

Babe Ruth

Ohtani is often compared to Babe Ruth. Ruth, born in 1895,
played for the MLB from 1914–1935. Over 22 seasons, he hit
714 home runs. He led the New York Yankees to four World
Championships. Many say he changed the game of baseball with
powerful hitting. He started out as a pitcher and outfielder but
chose to focus on the outfield with his powerful batting.

CHAPTER FIVE

BEYOND BASEBALL

Ohtani is known for excelling on and off the field. In 2021, Ohtani gave his $150,000 earnings from the Home Run Derby to about 30 Angels support staff. He is known for cleaning up after himself in the dugout. That year, Ohtani was also named one of the 100 most influential people of 2021 by *TIME* magazine. He is one of just two MLB players to have received the honor. Former MLB player Alex Rodriguez told *TIME*, "Not only is he incredible on the field, but off the field he's a gentleman. His teammates have only good things to say about Shohei, and he is great with the media and fans too."

〉〉〉 Alex Rodriguez

Within a year, Ohtani went from $6 million to $20 million in **endorsements** from both American and Japanese companies. By 2022, he broke the record for the MLB player with the most endorsements, with a whopping 17! His success led 22 Japanese brands to advertise at Angel Stadium as well.

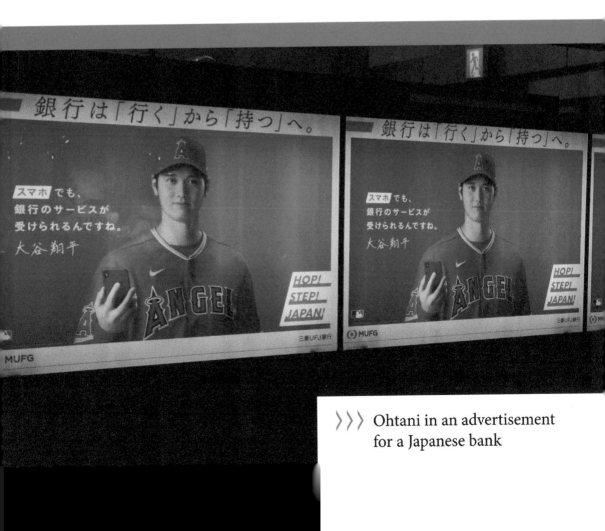

⟩⟩⟩ Ohtani in an advertisement for a Japanese bank

The MLB also created marketing campaigns around Ohtani. During the 2021 All-Star Game, the MLB celebrated "Sho-Time." The 30-second video showcased Ohtani as a "phenom," "speedster," and "global superstar."

The Angels' organization also hoped to draw more fans to the ballpark with "Ohtani Mania."

Many fans are coming to see Ohtani play. The Angels director of ticket sales, Jim Pannetta, said, "Shohei did something in baseball that's never been done, and we just want to get people out to see him." In the 2022 season, the Angels stadium gave away Ohtani tote bags, T-shirts, snow globes, and three different bobbleheads.

Ohtani merchandise in the Angel Stadium gift shop

>>> Shohei Ohtani's American League MVP bobblehead

FACT

On Star Wars night, the Angels stadium passed out Ohtani-Wan Kenobi bobbleheads.

Many say that Ohtani is the greatest thing to happen to baseball in 100 years. His goal is to continue playing his best while touching lives along the way. "The only thing I can promise you is that I'm going to play as hard as I can all the time and give 100 percent," said Ohtani. "Hopefully, by doing that, I can inspire numerous people, maybe in their personal life, if they're having other issues, and cheer them up by watching me play. That would probably be the most honorable thing about playing baseball."

〉〉〉 Ohtani slides into second base in a game against the Twins on July 25, 2021.

TIMELINE

1994 Shohei Ohtani is born on July 5 in Mizusawa (present-day Ōshū), Japan

2002 Ohtani begins playing baseball at age 8.

2010 Ohtani plays baseball for the Hanamaki Higashi High School in Iwate, Japan.

2012 Ohtani is drafted by the Hokkaido Nippon-Ham Fighters as the overall number-one pick.

2016 Ohtani contributes to the Nippon-Ham Fighters win of the the Japan Series. He makes history by being named the Pacific League's best pitcher and designated hitter.

2017 Ohtani enters the MLB and signs with the Los Angeles Angels.

2018 Ohtani is named MLB American League Rookie of the Year.

2018 Ohtani undergoes Tommy John elbow surgery.

2021 Ohtani is the first MLB player to both pitch and hit in the All-Star Game.

2021 Ohtani voted American League Most Valuable Player.

2022 Ohtani hits his first career grand slam.

GLOSSARY

COVID-19 PANDEMIC (KOH-vid nine-TEEN pan-DEM-ik)—a very contagious, sometimes deadly, virus that spread worldwide in 2020

DEBUT (DAY-byoo)—a player's first game

ENDORSEMENT (in-DORS-muhnt)—when someone sponsors a product by appearing in advertisements or on the product in exchange for money and perks

FREE AGENT (FREE AY-juhnt)—a player who is free to sign with any team

INDUCT (in-DUHKT)—to formally admit someone into a position or place of honor

LIGAMENT (LIG-uh-muhnt)—a band of tissue that connects bones to bones

PANDEMIC (pan-DEM-ik)—a disease that spreads over a wide area and affects many people

RECRUIT (ri-KROOT)—to ask someone to join something

REHAB (REE-hab)—to restore to its former use

ROOKIE (RUK-ee)—a first-year player

UNANIMOUS (yoo-NAN-uh-muhss)—agreed on by everyone

READ MORE

Burrel, Dean. *Baseball Biographies for Kids: The Greatest Players from the 1960s to Today.* Emeryville, CA: Rockridge Press, 2020.

Fishman, John M. *Shohei Ohtani.* Minneapolis: Lerner Publications, 2022.

Jacobs, Greg. *The Everything Kids' Baseball Book, 11th Edition: From Baseball's History to Today's Favorite Players-With Lots of Home Run Fun in Between!* New York: Simon & Schuster, 2020.

INTERNET SITES

MLB Kids Website
mlb.com/fans/kids

National Baseball Hall of Fame
baseballhall.org/

Sports Illustrated for Kids Baseball
sikids.com/baseball

INDEX

AUTHOR BIO

Cheryl Kim is an elementary teacher from California currently teaching at an international school in Thailand. She lives in Chiang Mai with her husband Brandon and sons Nathanael and Zachary.